MW01177818

The purpose of this book is to show children
that our Christmas traditions are rooted
in our faith in Jesus Christ, God's only Son.
The Christmas season is a perfect time
to discuss with children the blessings of our faith.

Christmas
The Birthday of Christ

by
Patricia Richardson Mattozzi

The Regina Press New York

Published by The Regina Press, Melville, NY 11747

ISBN 088271 493 7

What if Jesus had not come
to be the Christ, God's only Son?

Christmas simply would be not be
a holiday for you and me.

There would be no Christmas cards to send —
with our love and joy...

no stockings would be filled
for good little girls and boys.

There would be no holiday goodies
to decorate and bake...

no colored lights on Christmas trees,
no ornaments to make!

We wouldn't wait and listen
on a midnight clear
for Santa and his sleigh
and his eight reindeer.

There would be no packages
to mail to friends far away,
no gifts to share with loved ones
on Merry Christmas Day.

There would be no church for prayer,
no carols we could sing...

no manger with the shepherds,
no worship by the kings.

Praise God that Baby Jesus
was born on Christmas Day...

We can celebrate His birth
in so many different ways!

And when Christmas Day is over
and a brand New Year I see...
I thank God for sending Jesus
into the world for me!

Jesus said:
I came that they might have life
and they might have it more abundantly.

John 10:10